Bum *Town*

Tony
Fitzpatrick

TIA CHUCHA PRESS
CHICAGO AND LOS ANGELES

Cover and book design by Jane Brunette

Published by Tia Chucha Press
Luis Rodriguez, Founder and Editorial Director

For information write to
Tia Chucha Press
The Guild Complex
1212 N. Ashland Ave.
Chicago IL 60622.

Distributed by Northwestern University Press;
for orders, call 1-800-621-2736.

Guild Complex publishes this book with the
much appreciated financial support of the
Richard H. Driehaus Foundation, the National
Endowment for the Arts, The Illinois Arts
Council, the John D. and Catherine T.
MacArthur Foundation, the WPWR-TV Channel
50 Foundation, the Sara Lee Foundation, and
other donors.

acknowledgments

Thank you, Teresa Mucha, you're the greatest—
nobody compares to you.

Thank you: Reg Gibbons, for your help, guidance
and largeness of heart; Luis Rodriguez
and Julie Parson-Nesbitt my old friends and new
publishers; the Guild Complex—for
initiating a white-trash outreach program;
Michael Warr—for knowing nothing about
baseball and everything about being a friend.
Thank you to my everyday coconspirators in
fun and covert activities—they are: Teddy
Varndell, Joe Silverberg, Marc Hauser, Joe
Tabet, Leah Missbach, Jessica Feith, Adrienne
Armstrong, Don Degrazia, John
McNaughton, the whole wait-staff at Toast
(Damen Avenue), Zak Mucha, Drew and
Michelle Jahelka, Hillel and MaryJo Levin,
Padmaja Manevikar. A very special thank-you to
Steve Earle, fearless heart. And to Mickey Cartin.
He knows why.

Special thank-you to Elizabeth Taylor of the
Chicago Tribune and Dave (nothing good ever
happened before midnight) Hoekstra of the
Chicago Sun-Times, and especially Rick Kogan,
whom my mom falsely credits with being a good
influence.

I thank my brothers, sisters, all their children, my
Aunt Mary, my Uncle Gene, my cousins—you
get the idea.

I thank my wife Michele the most—who has
made my journey joyful and full of love, and my
kids Max and Gaby—I love you little wise guys
more than life itself.

TO MY MOTHER, ANNAMAE,
WHO LIT THE WAY FOR A FATHER AND SON

He borrows moonlight
For this journey of a million miles.

—Saikaku

. . .

You are
To us:
The Past.

RUNNER
On the prairie
Good-by.

—Carl Sandburg

Bum Town

From 79th Street
Southworks flexed its

Muscle of light,
An infinite halo
Of orange and white;
Like they had captured
The sun
In four steel walls . . .
And they had.

Its mighty slag
Filled potholes on
Torrance Avenue clear down

To the Calumet River,
Where it lay in heaps
Like dirty linen.

I could hear the lapping
Of black water
And the grinding of
Rivers and rails.
On hot days
I could smell the yards,
Blood and meat and iron
Carried on the breeze
Like new curses.

I could feel the
Murderous rumble
Of my Dad's Oldsmobile
Weaving in and out of
Night and day traffic
Like a gull in the wind.
He'd tool up Western Avenue
And remind me that the

Green Hornet streetcars
Once rode the longest line
In the world,
Right here.

And Western would trot out
Its goods: grocerías
And tarted-up car lots
Lit up like the Carnival
Or Saint Rocco's day,
Used cars and short skirts,
Hot-dog joints and the union hall.
Then like now
Western looks like the girl
With too much eye-shadow.

In the scrap lots,

Bottle-gangs of invisible men
Drank pints of Mad-dog
While burning garbage
Kept them warm. They seemed to
Disappear into the smoke
One orange ember
At a time.
Like human coal
The city shovels
Into itself.

My Dad would fuss
With the radio until

The voice of Bob Elson
Filled the Olds with the
Sox lineup: Staley, Landis,
Rivera, Aparicio, Fox, Pierce,
And Lollar . . .
A couple of years past Go-Go
But game enough
For Bridgeport's
Strutting beer-bellies
And crewcuts.

The Comiskey crowd
Would file in, scowl to scowl,
Elbow to elbow in the shrine
The old Roman built
On the backs of underpaid
Ballplayers. So cheap was Comiskey
That he'd only launder uniforms
Once a week.
"Tighter than a bag of assholes,"
My father would say.

The White Sox would
Sail on the
Ancient knuckleball of
Hoyt Wilhelm,
Ace fireman of his time.
He was one of those guys
Who was old even when
He was young.
He'd stare down the 9th inning
With the patience of a
Carrion bird
And we the people
Would wait him out
For the
Secret.

I wanted to know
The secrets and pacts
Of slaughtered cattle
And exploding scoreboards,
Of my mother's and father's
Great romance on 72nd Street,
Where he would get on the streetcar
And then two others
To Austin Boulevard
Just to
Look at her.
I wanted the city
To give up its litanies
Of the living
And the dead.

The dead still walk

This city.
I dreamt once that
Children burnt in a fire,
With only their arms for blankets,
Sang in the frozen night
Outside a church
While angels wept down upon them.
92 children howled and screamed
Like dying animals,
Singing for God
To let them
Back in.

The dead still talk
In this city.
My Dad drove an ambulance
For Thompson Funeral Parlor
At 79th and Ellis
And sometimes the dead
Spoke to him through
The radio

Or called him on the phone
But when he turned
On the TV
They'd only
Stare back
Waving silently
In black and white.

The Irish dead still talk
A lot in this city.
The fog is like cigar smoke
At the foot of the lake,
And Richard J. Daley
Could always see through
The smoke.
Every wink, every nod,
Every smirk
Turned into highways,
Skyscrapers and bridges.
"I'm a kid from the stockyards—
I'll stand with you."
And he did.

Then the Irish
Licked the frosting,
Ate the cake
And sold the
Plate.

Who built the pyramids?
Mayor Daley built the pyramids.

The white-haired poet said,

"The people know what
The land knows."
Not true with this city.
This city knows itself by
Its noises, like those whistles
Only dogs can hear.
The city hears the cries of
Battered wives, the wailing of
Underweight babies
And the euphony of
Children circling an opened
Hydrant.

This city knows, it can hear itself
In sirens and tow-trucks,
Broken bottles and the mewling
Of strays.
The needing,
The wanting
And the pleading
Thrum in
Every window.

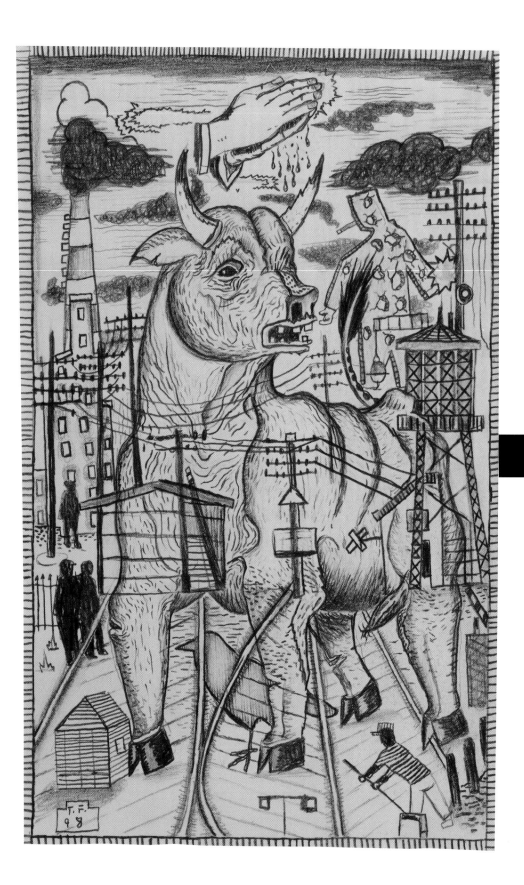

Under the constellations
My Dad buys me an Italian ice
With lemon peels I can taste
The sun in.
The smelt are running
Off Montrose Harbor.
My Dad points to the North Star
And shows me how boats
Box the compass
Around it.
Under the dock the smelt
Are a whir of silvery light—
As indecipherable as
The tails of
Comets.

On the 4th of July

I lie on a blanket
And the sky rips open
With fire
And white tendrils
Of hope.
My Dad lights
His cigar with a
Road flare
And tells me
About Okinawa—
Tracers and bullets,
Sailors and marines—
When he thought
Every night was
Independence Day.
Only to wake up
The next morning

And see bodies strewn
On the beach,
Mile after whistling mile.
Marines and sailors
Felt the sea
Roll and swell
Under their legs.
Lengthening shadows
Mocked them from
The deck of the
U. S. S. Noble.
My Dad and every other
19-year-old
On this ship
Wanted only to be beyond
The bloodshed,
The blank, dead faces.
Our guys,
Their guys,
In the blood and sand
He couldn't tell one
From another.

My Dad looked up
At the rockets,
A red one burst
Around his head
Like a nimbus
Of bloody light
And his shadow
Falls across my face
Like a shroud
Made from ghosts.

He rolls the Olds
Slowly
Along the South Shore
Tracks.
Squinting his eyes
He looks for the smoke
That becomes his brother
Raymond.
Up ahead a small boy
With one leg
Sits on a switchman's box
Eating from a sticky
Carton of Cracker Jack.
My Dad's lips move
Without speaking
As he carries Raymond
To the car.

I look at the boy
In the back seat—
His skin is as white
As alabaster
Under a shock of black hair,
His leg is
A ragged stump,
Hastily sutured
Decades ago,
When Raymond died
Trying to hop
A freight train.
The small ghost
Does not speak,
But breaks into
A crooked grin
As he holds out his
Cracker Jack
To me.
"This is your Uncle Ray—
Sometimes he comes with me."
I nod my head
And smile back at
Raymond.

My Dad drives to
73rd and Racine:
Elmer Kosack's grocery
Is long gone
As are the
Black licorice pipes
And Bull Durham
Tobacco pouches.
My Dad and Raymond
Look with wide eyes
At their first home.
It is peopled
With other people
Who speak a
Different language,
Eat a different food,
And know nothing
Of Saint Brendan's
Or Doolan's juke bar,
Nor the mighty
Orange and Black
Of Leo High School.
My Dad and Raymond
Look to each other
As if looking into
Distant mirrors.

There is death

In our car,
And there is birth;
And neither
My Dad nor Raymond
Knows which.
They just know
It is one
Or the other.

There is death
In this neighborhood—
Insurance fires,
The breaking apart
And hauling away,
The bitter words
And tears
And the bigotries
As ancient
As amber
And toxic as
Mercury.
Hate-filled words
Wielded like a razor:
Polak
Nigger
Spic
Cracker
Loogan
Kike
Dago . . .

The words
We carved
Into one another's
Hearts
Like numbers
On a grave stone.
The communion
Of hatreds
Passed among
Priest and penitent
Alike.

There is birth

In this neighborhood.
Lily of the Valley
Still grows
In the shade
Between homes.
Small girls
With beaded hair
Jump rope
Double-Dutch style,
Their voices
A joyful music
Hurled around
The sun and back.
There are tamales
Made in the husk for a dollar.

And Lotto tickets—
The prayer-wheel
Of poverty
Sold to the suckers
Like holy cards.
Yes, the lottery:
The toothless man
Yells "It's like pickin'
God's pocket."
There are Cotillions,
And the Good Humor man
Selling Bomb-Pops
And Wha-Hoo bars.
There is salsa
And gut-bucket
Guitar blues,
The west-side
Kind.
These guitars
Hold
All of the voices
And then some.
So we the people
Listen, and sway
And sing to
Ourselves
Of mercy
And medicine
And each other.

My Dad stops the Olds
At Mt. Olivet cemetery.
It is nearly dark
And Raymond
Must return.
My Dad sets Raymond at
The gates
And walks away,
His lips moving
Without speaking.
His hand trembles
As he twists the
Ignition key
And for the first time
I witness my Dad's
Covenant
With ghosts.

As we drive by

The Stadium
My Dad tells
Me about
The Zale-Graziano
Fight. Of how
Tony Zale of Gary
Indiana and
Rocky Graziano
Of the Bronx
Nearly murdered

One another
On a hot night in
The summer of 1946
While every radio
In America shook
With static
At every punch.

The crowd at the
Stadium was a writhing
Animal of arms, mouths
And sweat, roaring
Like a wounded
Monster,
For this night
They were not
Meat packers,
Brickyard jockeys,
Cops or pothole-
Fillers—

On this night
They were the
Animal itself,
Yelling for a murder they
Were entitled to.
They roared for
Their corner.
Their boy.
Their displaced
Person's dream.
Their lumpen pound of
Blood and muscle.

When Zale was
KO'd
In the 6th
His eyes looked
Like blackened
Candle wicks.

My Dad eases
The Olds into a
Corner parking
Spot outside
Slotkowski's at
18th and Halsted.
He gets some brats
And a smoked ham
Cured with honey—
Irish steak for
Sunday.
My Dad hands me
A dried beef stick
And as I eat it my
Head sweats and
The scent of garlic
Fills the Olds
Like ether.
We roll down
The windows,
My Dad laughing
That we smell
Like 10 pounds of skunk
In a 5-pound bag.

Along 115th Street

My Dad searches
Out the
Tracks and the
Yesterday people
Who still walk
Between the trains,
The ashen men looking
For returnable bottles
And tailor-made
Cigarette butts.

And once again
The invisible men
Remake themselves
With fog and broken
Glass while gathered
Like the bastard children
Of locomotive smoke
Or the spirits of
Murdered Indians
And faceless gangsters.

As I fall asleep

In the front seat
I lean against my Dad
And the last thing
He tells me is
That men used to hop
The trains to get lost
And they hopped off 'em
Hoping to be found
But he can't tell who
Is who, he just knows
Men need one
Or the other.

Going South
In my sleep,
Saint Therese watches us
From the dashboard.
Her beatific smile glowing,
Her Carmelite shawl opens
With a shower of roses.
And outside
White petals float
On a billowed wind
Across Stony Island Avenue.
We watch,
Nearer to God's heart.
We forgo all other
Ecstasies,
All other evidence
And all other prayers.